A
Beginner's Guide
to Aviation

David F. Leuchter

Printed in the United States of America

The Leuchter Co. LLC

2028 E. Ben White Blvd. Ste. 240-28104

Austin, TX, 78741

www.theleuchter.co

ISBN: 978-1-542-46563-2

To God, my wife & my family.

iv

12:2

Table of Contents

Chapter 1:
Getting started

Aviation remains an idealistic frontier for many people. It is free and unfettered, genuine and pure. There is really no comparison to the feeling of being alone in an airplane for the first time. People who have done it can try to describe it, but words cannot convey the feeling of this experience. Perhaps you simply want to experience for yourself, tired of always being a passenger and never the driver. Or maybe you need an economical means of traveling for business (and pleasure). There is also the camp of people seeking a career in aviation, specifically, pilot. Whatever the reason is for you pursuing aviation, you need a solid entry strategy. Flying is a commodity that has a significant buy-in cost; you are going to have a significant outlay of cash in order to do anything. But how much you spend can be controlled to a certain extent. A person can, and often will, throw a significant amount of money at flying and certainly maintains the ability to walk away with very little for their efforts. Sadly, numerous student pilots walk away from flying before they ever receive their license, and a huge number of already licensed pilots allow their currency to lapse. According to the Aircraft Owners and Pilots Association (AOPA), some 500,000 licensed pilots are presently non-current, shelving their licenses for one reason or another[1], cost generally being a likely contributor to the lack of activity. Time is another contributing factor; keeping current and staying up to speed on the learning curve of aviation takes time and effort. In order to stay safe and be proficient in the

---

[1] AOPA Rusty Pilot program https://www.aopa.org/training-and-safety/lapsed-pilots/rusty-pilots.

craft, you have to spend time in the air. Time is money, as is said, and you are going to pay for your proficiency.

There are a lot of options available for the non-pilot to break into flying, and the first step you should take is determining exactly what it is that you want to do with it. Not all licenses, or ratings as they are known, are built the same. And in fact, some flying machines and categories require no license (or training) at all, although training is highly recommended.

The simplest variety of aircraft available are those which fall in the category of ultralights, which are governed by Title 14 of the Code of Federal Regulations (CFR), Part 103[2], which is commonly known as just "Part 103". Ultralights are very small (powered machines must be under 254lbs empty), very slow (cannot exceed fifty-five knots), and possess a very short range (five-gallon maximum fuel capacity).

Ultralight Trike
Author: Oliver Ren / CC 3.0

Ultralights encompass a broad array of aircraft configurations, including traditional three-axis aircraft, weight-shift aircraft, powered parachutes, gyroplanes, and even helicopters. These are intended to be used for fun, and their usefulness is really very limited. But if you just want to take off from a small grass field and fly around to feel the wind in your face, then these might be worth a look. Since they are not registered by the Federal Aviation Administration

---

[2] http://www.ecfr.gov/cgi-bin/text-idx?rgn=div5&node=14:2.0.1.3.16

(FAA), they are not subject to the rigorous maintenance requirements imposed on certified aircraft. However, this does come at some cost to the oversight of their inherent reliability, but the ultralight community has come a long way since its inception in the 1970s where fatal accidents were not necessarily uncommon.

Conventional tri-axis designs are still widely available in the ultralight market, but the weight-shift trikes and powered parachutes are very popular as well. A big reason that this can be attributed to is the simplicity of operation, particularly the powered parachutes. Licensed fixed wing pilots may lean towards traditional designs, but weight-shift and powered parachutes are very enticing to people with no flying experience. There is no need to understand the relationship between the axis of flight, and the coordination between pitch, bank, and yaw as they relate to elevators, ailerons, and rudders. Weight-shift machines essentially go where you point the wing, and powered parachutes have the added benefit of an existing safety device which is constantly deployed.

One of the real significant limitations of the ultralight is its limitation to a single seat. Ultralights have no provision for passengers, so ultralight pilots are going to fly solo. Also, you must take into consideration your own size as the pilot. For instance, a 245lb pilot weighs nearly as much as the aircraft itself, so that might not be a realistic option for all pilots. All in all, if slow, low altitude scenic pleasure flying is your prerogative, maybe you should give one of the avenues of ultralights a look. The major upswing to this category of flying is the very low cost. The machines can regularly be had used for $5,000 or less, with a lot of new machines still tipping the scales significantly under $10,000. There is no licensing requirement, and no registration requirement for the vehicle, so it would just be purchase cost and insurance. They used very little fuel, so that is a negligible factor.

The Sport Pilot certificate is the next progression logically from ultralight aircraft. The Sport Pilot certification is fairly new, having come into existence in September 2004. The purpose of the Sport Pilot certificate was to provide a simpler and quicker certification path for people seeking to fly a new segment of aircraft known as Light Sport Aircraft. These aircraft encompass a very broad range of aircraft including airplanes, gyroplanes, airships (blimps), balloons, weight-shift, gliders, and powered parachutes.

Skyleader 'GP One'
Author: B H Conway / CC 4.0

The reality had long set in that ultralights were good for little more than local sightseeing, and only for the pilot. The limitations made on the aircraft are so restrictive that there is little value in owning or flying one. Light Sport aircraft, as defined in 14 CFR Part 1.1, allow a more capable aircraft while staying in the spirit of the ultralight movement. The fore mentioned weight-shift "trikes" and powered parachutes are a natural platform to take a passenger, but could not under Part 103 rules to ultralights. The trikes and traditional airplanes falling under Part 103 rules could certainly stand to hold a little more fuel, have seating for one passenger, and cruise slightly faster without taking away from the simplicity of ultralights. In this, the Light Sport category was born. They are still small (1,320lbs and under), slow (120 knot maximum speed in level flight), and simple (fixed landing gear, fixed-pitch propeller).

In a rare case of sensibility, the FAA made a certificate to collaborate with the Light Sport Aircraft (LSA) category, since the existing recreational and private pilot certificates were more than was actually necessary for the LSAs on the market. Not only that, but those certificates are designed for fixed-wing airplane operations which many LSA operators may never even use. If you went on to earn a private pilot certificate, you would still need to backtrack and perform flight training in a trike or powered parachute, for instance. The Sport Pilot certificate allows prospective pilots to train in the specific platform for which they intend to fly. Since these aircraft are inherently simple, the Sport Pilot certificate has significantly lower requirements for minimum hours in training prior to granting the certificate. Where the private pilot has a minimum total hour requirement of 40 hours, the Sport Pilot requires only 20. Simple machines like the powered parachutes and trikes just do not require as much "stick time" to become proficient, but with simplicity come limitations.

Sport pilots are limited to daytime and Visual Flight Rules (VFR) operations, and may not operate in airspace requiring radio communication unless they have been specifically trained and endorsed by a Certified Flight Instructor (CFI). The Sport pilot may fly cross country in an LSA, although they may not fly about 2,000' Above Ground Level (AGL), which is fairly low. That being said, a lot of LSA are not geared towards anything besides low altitude flight to begin with, particularly powered parachutes.

A number of Experimental category, or "homebuilt" and "kit built" aircraft fall under the LSA umbrella, which has made it very attractive to this demographic. These aircraft, as the name suggest, are built either completely from scratch using a set of plans, or are delivered as a partially built kit with instructions from a factory. Many pilots of these aircraft intend to use them simply as a joyrider, and the vast majority of these designs are single- or dual-seat only, designed for simple, slow flight. This is not the universal case, as some of the kits are extremely complex and are very high performing airplanes upon completion. But the bulk of experimental category airplanes are designed with the intention of making aviation affordable to the every-man, and provide simple

Hummelbird Ultra Cruiser Landing
Author: Ahunt. / CC0 1.0

designs which are intended to be safe, cost-effective, and built in a reasonable period of time. A number of experimental designs, such as the Hummelbird[3] and the Volksplane VP-1[4] are specifically designed to use the ever plentiful and very inexpensive Volkswagen air cooled engines of Beetle fame. If you are handy and want to fly recreationally, this may very well be a route to consider. The cost cannot be beat, and if you do go ahead and build an airplane (over 51% of it), you may request a Repairman's Certificate from the FAA so that you may perform maintenance and repairs yourself rather than hiring a costly mechanic.

---

[3] http://www.flyhummel.com/
[4] http://www.evansair.com/

The final perk worth mentioning is that the Sport pilot certificate was the first FAA license which did not require pilots (including student pilots) to obtain a medical check-up from an FAA approved medical examiner. There is currently legislation which has passed that frees up private pilots from having to maintain a medical, but the FAA is still working the regulatory component of the law. Sport pilots are only required to maintain a valid state-issued driving license.

The recreational pilot certificate is an idea which never took off in the flying community. It was envisioned as a certificate that was cheaper to and quicker to obtain than the private pilot, but it came at the expense of limitations on what the pilot can operate and do. As with all pilot certificates, the limitations and restrictions are found in 14 CFR Part 61. In a nutshell, the recreational certificate limits the pilot to only one passenger (even in a four-seat aircraft), daytime visual flight only, flying an airplane of 180 horsepower or less, and may only operate within 50 nautical miles of the home airport.

This begs the question: why? The recreational certificate came long before Light Sport aircraft were a blip on anyone's radar. There were experimental category aircraft, but these were still lurking in the dark corners of respectability, basically as a niche community. So the FAA paired away some of the most useful features of the private pilot certificate, cut minimum flight training requirements by 25%, and packaged it up as the recreational pilot. My personal take on this is it fairly useless for practical uses, and it still costs a lot of money to obtain. If you decide to fly, you must accept that it comes with a large price tag. If you are committed to flying, you are committing yourself to a large expenditure no matter what so you may as well push forward to the private pilot. Of course, this advice is intended for anyone interested in the recreational versus private pilot certificates. If it works for your needs, the light sport is definitely the most cost-effective option out there to get you into a certified aircraft.

The private pilot certificate is certainly the most useful of the introductory licenses presently available, Given the time and resources, it would be in the pilots' best interest to earn this certificate. The private pilot has the ability to exercise every function of all the other subordinate certificates (ultralights, sport pilot, recreational pilot), and allows pilots to do much more. You may fly into any controlled airspace, so long as you abide by all applicable rules. You may fly cross-country and you may fly at night. In fact, you may do both if you wish. Also, this is the only basic license in which you may pursue an instrument rating later on.

The privileges of the private pilot are the defined in 14 Part 61 of the CFR. All pilots have an obligation to understand and heed these limitations, and pleading ignorance will not get high marks from the FAA should a pilot choose to ignore them. The basics are as follows:

- Certificate may be issued at age 17 for powered aircraft, 16 for gliders and balloons.

- Private pilots may fly cross country.

- Private pilots may fly at night.

- Private pilots may fly for business purposes, but may not charge for services rendered as a private pilot.

There are myriad of additional "endorsements" to add on to the private pilot certificate, and its useful value is almost unlimited. Common endorsements include tailwheel, complex airplane, high-performance, and pressurized aircraft. Tailwheel is just as it sounds; it is configured using a tailwheel rather than the ubiquitous

Piper PA-46
Author: Matti Blume / CC 4.0

tricycle configuration commonly found on general aviation aircraft. Complex airplane are airplanes with a

Eclipse 550 LX
Author: Robert Frola / GNU

variable-pitch propeller, flaps, and retractable landing gear. High-performance airplanes are an airplane with 200 horsepower or more. This can be confusing because a high-performance airplane does not necessarily meet the criteria of complex, and vice versa. Pressurized aircraft would be those which are intended to be flown at high altitudes and have a completed sealed and pressurized cabin.

Ratings are another type of additional credentialing which you may add onto an existing license. The two most common ratings to add to the useful private pilot license are an instrument rating, and the multi-engine rating. The names are fairly self-explanatory; the instrument rating allows you to fly during Instrument Meteorological Conditions (IMC), or to fly on an instrument flight plan during any conditions. The multi-engine rating allows you to operate aircraft having more than one engine.

More than any other rating or endorsement that a pilot may opt for upon receiving their private pilot license, there is none more valuable than the instrument rating. This rating provides tremendous advantages in safety, economy, and usefulness over any other. Looking objectively, this is very little use for a multi-engine rating, complex endorsement, or high-performance endorsement without the instrument rating because this aircraft is all tailored to conditions and uses favorable for instrument flying. There is simply no need for the speed, altitude, and longevity of high-performance, complex, or multi-engine airplanes if you are grounded because of clouds. Additionally, the instrument rating and subsequent instrument flight plans make transiting congested airspace so much faster and easier when the onus of responsibility falls on the air traffic controller to provide separation and vectoring rather than the pilot in command (PIC). When a flight is filed as an instrument flight plan, whether the weather is IMC or not, air traffic control (ATC) provides separation, sequencing, and navigational directing (vectoring) to the pilot from the moment that the flight plan is activated until it is terminated. ATC provides very specific directions regarding route of flight, frequencies, and altitude on the clearance, and specific

Seair Seaplane
Author: Seair Seaplanes / CC

altitudes, headings, and follow-on information once a release is issued.

It would be unfair to not add something about the Seaplane rating. For much of the lower 48 states, this rating is quite limited in usefulness. However, if you happen to live in a coastal area, or live and plan to fly in Alaska, then you may want (or need) to consider this rating. Seaplanes come in two basic forms: standard aircraft, floatplanes, retrofitted with pontoon-style floats, and then flying boats, which are designed and constructed specifically to land in the water and float much like a boat. The fuselage of these flying boats is shaped and built similarly to a boat, so it operates directly on the water as a boat would. Seaplanes are further broken down into a subclass known as amphibious aircraft if they are equipped with a retractable wheeled landing gear. While this sounds ideal for a recreational aircraft application, it certainly has some drawbacks. First and foremost is drag. The pontoon floats add a tremendous amount of drag to an aircraft, substantially reducing efficiency. Remember, drag is the bane of aerodynamic efficiency, which is the essential appeal of retractable-gear aircraft. Second, once floats are on an aircraft, it is a permanent affair. They are attached very different structurally from standard landing gear configurations (with the exception of a few very small experimental aircraft which use inflatable floats), to account for the center of gravity (CG) change from adding large, heavy surfaces to the exterior of the aircraft.

Flying boats tend offer an aerodynamic advantage over floatplanes, but they make up for it in cost. They are uncommon, which leads to higher pricing. They are definitely a niche aircraft, and will require extensive inspection for water tightness, corrosion, and the other sundry of issues surrounding keeping an airplane

Catalina Flying Boat
Author: Rob Mitchell / CC 1.0

in water for extended periods of time. Unless you plan on operating on water regularly, the only purpose for obtaining a seaplane rating is essentially bragging rights, or to challenge your piloting skills.

Chapter 2:
<u>Choosing Flight Instruction</u>

Now that you have some exposure to what options are available to exercise as a pilot, it is time to start thinking about where you want to invest your hard-earned dollars in training. This should be easy enough; just get on Google and search the nearest flight school and bring your credit card. This obviously faux pas is exactly what you should not do, unless you are in the business of losing money and enjoying disappointment. Yes, the local FBO will gladly take your money, and it really may be the best option suited for your goals. Or it may be the only option available due to geographic availability. There usually are flight schools at most small airports, so if you live rurally this might be your only option.

At the opposite end of the spectrum are professional flight schools, which often come in two forms. The first are programs as part of an accredited university, such as the well-known programs as Kansas State University, North Dakota State University, and the University of Central Missouri to name a few. These are programs often associated with a specific two- or four-year degree program. This can be a good option for career-oriented students of aviation who are of traditional college age. The reality is that you cannot qualify to be a military pilot without a four-year degree, and you will not get a look by the airlines either without a four-year degree.

There are also several well-known flight schools that specialize in taking zero-time or low-time pilots and putting them on a fast track to getting the requisite hours and ratings to break into the profession. The most prominent of these schools are ATP Flight School, and Flight Safety International, although there are several others to choose from. The way it works is that, assuming you are accepted, you go to one of their regional training centers for about six months where you will earn all of the necessary ratings and endorsements to get a job flying. Also, most of these big schools have well-established job placement services in-house, often with guaranteed positions as CFIs to build time to get into airline minimums. If you are looking for a career change and already have a degree, this is certainly the fastest (and perhaps most surefire) way to get into the cockpit. But it comes with a hefty fee. ATP Flight School is currently charging $80,995[5] for their Airline Career Pilot program, which is the 270-day in-house program.

Before anyone goes off to write that big check for the all-in-one pilot starter package, take a moment to understand the key differences in each type of program. The first program going under the microscope is the small Mom-n'-Pop flight schools at the local airport. These schools, often run in conjunction with the Fixed Base Operator (FBO), fall under the jurisdiction of 14 CFR Part 61. These means that the rules governing these flight schools under delineated under Title 14 of the Code of Federal Regulations, in chapter I, part 61. Most people shorten this to simply Part 61.

Part 61 schools are held to a less rigid standard in their teaching techniques and curriculum. They do not even have to hold a dedicated ground school for student pilots! Instead, the ground school portion is generally taught on a lesson-by-lesson basis in conjunction with a

---

[5] Current as of March, 2020.
www.atpflightschools.com/airline-career-pilot-program/index.html

flying lesson. Generally speaking, these schools (as well as flying clubs) are not geared towards teaching student pilots for professional aviation. These are recreationally inclined with the pleasure seeker in mind and weekend flyer in mind. However, this is not to say that a pilot could not earn all necessary ratings to become a successful commercial pilot through a Part 61 flight school, but there are some potential drawbacks.

Part 141 schools are monitored very closely, allowing very little flexibility in their training regimen. The balance to this is that Part 141 schools allow pilots to earn ratings in significantly less time that their Part 61 counterparts. For instance, a student pilot at a Part 141 school may earn their private pilot certificate in 35 hours vice the Part 61 minimum of 40 hours. The commercial rating is even more drastic, drawn down to 190-hour minimum in Part 141 from 250 hours in Part 61. As the adage goes, time is money, and this is never truer than in regard to flight hours. Take a Cessna 172 for instance, the gold standard for most flight training, running $150 per hour (not an exaggeration). In shaving off sixty flight hours, you

Cessna 172
Author: Eddie Maloney / CC 2.0

can potentially save almost $9,200 on minimum time towards the commercial certificate. This might be somewhat misleading, though. Yes, it may cost more to attain a commercial certificate by going straight through the hours required if your only goal is to hit the water mark. A lot of pilots fly for personal business of pleasure, so it may not take much time to get to the 250-hour maxim should they be interested in commercial aviation. Of course, it is fair to assume that a pilot with the financial ability or necessity to fly for personal business may not be interested in starting at the bottom of the totem in commercial aviation.

Part 141 flight schools have one very specific purpose, and that is building commercial pilots. Their curriculum is rigid, their training methods are strict (and strictly monitored), and there are very specific benchmarks to be met at specific points in the training cycle. As such, they are able to meet milestones in a shorter period of flight hours. Also, students of these schools will fly nearly daily, keeping their skills sharp. Flying is a skillset that is easily tarnished without practice, so following a training plan that requires constant flying and airmanship does reduce the cumulative hours necessary to master certain skills.

From the perspective of mere convenience and ease of process, these cannot be beat. They are eligible generally for student aid, so once a student is funded they quickly find themselves on the fast track to a career in flying. If a pilot were to choose to proceed at a Part 61 school, they will likely have to do so with their own cash flow so the rate of instruction will be regulated accordingly. But, if you fly often and are building hours outside of the academic environment this may work just fine.

While looking at this, the cost seems truly staggering. A Part 141 program which lasts six months may cost more than a four-year education does at many universities. Part 61 schools may end up costing about the same or a little less, but are dependent upon the pilot having the ability afford the instruction on the front-side of training, rather than the back-side. This all sounds somewhat bleak, but there are actually some options out there which can help to reduce the cost of instruction.

One option for reducing the cost of flying is to actually purchase a portion of an airplane, which is called fractional ownership. In doing this, several people will purchase a portion of an airplane, including a pro rata share of maintenance as well. This is an effective strategy for people who need to build substantial flight hours and plan to fly often. The cost per hour is generally quite a bit lower in a fractional ownership over renting because there is no profit margin to be had. Also, if only three people are operating the airplane there is probably going to be less of a challenge to schedule the airplane for flight as opposed to a flight school or FBO where the airplane is being operated most of the day. Personally owned (including fractional ownerships) airplane are also generally much nicer in-and-out than rentals.

The reason for cost reduction is due in large part to the cost sharing or regularly scheduled maintenance and inspections. For example, every airplane must have an annual inspection conducted by a certified Airframe and Powerplant (A&P) mechanic, which must be signed off by an Inspection Authority (IA) A&P. Assuming nothing major is found during the inspection, these are still expensive (think a thousand dollars minimum). But airplanes are usually old, so seldom is an inspection conducted that finds nothing. But in addition to the annual inspection, airplanes owned by flight schools with the expressed purpose of flight training must have an additional inspection conducted every 100 hours. These costs add up quickly, and that is all reflected in the rental fee. Fractionally-owned airplanes are usually not used for the purpose of flight instruction, so the owners are able to get out from under the 100-hour inspection requirement, which does save several thousand dollars per year. Bear in mind that at the end of the day, the purpose of a flight school/FBO is still to turn a profit so the hourly rate for rental has a lot of overhead costs. The best part of the fractional ownership is that you can always sell your portion if it becomes too burdensome or just unnecessary.

If you want to fly on the cheap(er) and want to own, but don't like the thought of sharing, then perhaps a strong contender really is the experimental aircraft market. Often, these come in the form of a kit that is all-inclusive. There are varying degrees of complexity in kit-built aircraft, and incredibly varied levels of performance. As such, there is a huge variance in cost between the most basic of aircraft, up through very high performance machines. It is realistic to expect to pay under $30,000 for a decent two-place kit built aircraft with basic instrumentation. This may sound like a lot of money, but look at some of the variables:

- The end resultant airplane will be essentially a factory new aircraft with zero hours. Factory-new, certified airplanes routinely cost well over $100,000. For a similar price point, you will likely be purchasing a very-used, simple trainer aircraft, often having well over 5,000 hours logged on the airframe.

- If you construct 51% or more of the aircraft, the FAA can grant you a Repairman's certificate, allowing you, the builder, to legally conduct all of your own maintenance, instead of having to hire a very costly A&P mechanic to do the work. This is worth thousands of dollars, and not just in the distant future either. An annual inspection can cost well over $1,000 every year, so this saving would be felt in the first year of ownership.

If the thought of ownership seems a bridge too far at this point in time, then there still some other options for lower-cost flying. Flying clubs are a very common fixture across America's airports, and for very good reasons. According to the Aircraft Owner and Pilot Association (AOPA), fully 55% of active pilots are members of a flying club[6]. Because a flying club is a community organization, i.e., a non-profit, which allows for a sharing of expenses over a relatively large number of people versus the very narrow expense of personal ownership. To be very clear, the local flight center at the average small airport is NOT a flying club. These flight centers are absolutely interested in making a profit, and with that knowledge is the reality that aircraft and instructors may lack in quality for the necessity of the company getting the absolute most out of each. Every second an aircraft is down for maintenance is a second that asset is costing money rather than earning it. This is a generality, not a concrete reality applicable to every flight center, but keep it in mind. Oftentimes the patience and virtue which a pilot will find in a flying club is lost in the staff of a flight center because of the mission of the organization. Flying clubs exist to share the thrill and joy of flight, and their founding members and leadership should hopefully be the embodiment of this truth. Flight centers are for-profit, and a lot of their instructors work there with the expressed purpose of time-building to get a look by the airlines. This results in a very high turnover rate, and these instructors by design will likely have less cumulative experience (not to mention less life experience; an irreplaceable

---

[6] AOPA, March 2020

intangible factor) than an instructor who teaches for love of the craft rather than monetary gain.

Outside of the cost advantages and increased quality of equipment in being a flying club member, there are certain intrinsic values which cannot be valued in monetary terms. Generally, the bylaws of a flying club stipulate meeting attendance requirements, etc., which usually does not evoke feelings of excitement or intrigue (unless someone brings donuts; that's a game changer). That being said, there are literally thousands and thousands of hours' worth of experience in most of these meetings, and the intended purpose of said meetings is to discuss fleet issues, training issues, safety issues, maintenance issues, and flying standard, as well as FAA regulatory updates and any number of other things. Why make a big deal about this? Because this is all free training. You get to pay exactly zero dollars to glean the wisdom from decades of experience of more seasoned pilots. It should be understood that there is no such thing as free in commercial flight training centers, regardless of whether they fall under Part 61 or 141 rules. All of your education will be hard scrabbled and has a definite fee. My experience with old pilots is that there is quite literally nothing that they would rather do than talk about flying. This is absolute gold, money in the bank. And they want to give it away to you!

Regardless of how or what you want to fly and do with flying, it really behooves a young pilot to join a flying club, if for no other reason than the free education. Remember, education does not necessarily come with a diploma. With absolute certainty, a young pilot will learn more in casual, comfortable conversation with a group of old, high-time pilots over coffee and bear claws than the same young pilot paying for his education from an accredited school. Just facts of life. If the hangar talk is that invaluable, just imagine what they can show you in the air. Not to mention the networking a pilot will be introduced to. This reminds me of a young pilot I know who currently flies turbine Thrush crop dusters for a living. A scant three years ago she was not even a pilot. After running into brick walls in several other ventures, she wanted to try her hand at something different. She had some money saved and joined the local flying club, where a senior member took her under his wing so-to-speak, and ultimately introduced her to the owner of a local aerial application (crop dusting) company. The owner talked with her, liked her, and offered her a job as a ground crew member, which is hardly glamorous. It involves a lot of tedious work, fueling and loading chemicals into the aircraft, from before dawn until dusk, during the entire warm-weather season. But he had the word of someone he trusted that she was a good, albeit inexperienced pilot. She proved herself in menial labor so the owner gave her the opportunity to fly for him as soon as she earned her commercial rating. Now she is racking up hundreds of hours doing a truly cool job, all because of local networking in a small-town flying club. Do not underestimate the power in a network of people.

The United States Air Force has an official auxiliary corps, known as the Civil Air Patrol. As an official auxiliary, the units are funded federally which means that they have flying hours available which need to be flown for the sake of proficiency, training, and real-world missions. The Civil Air Patrol, commonly referred to as 'The CAP', was conceived in the 1930s, as World War II loomed warily on the horizon. The idea was having a voluntary force of pilots who could conduct maritime patrols and non-combatant courier services in stateside service, missions which would unduly tax uniformed service members. Fast forward to present day and we see CAP serving primarily in the Search and Rescue capacity, disaster relief, humanitarian services, and even counternarcotic surveillance.

The CAP is a non-profit organization which is completely voluntary and all members are unpaid. So what exactly is the benefit to the private pilot? CAP requires a certain amount of qualified, current pilots who are willing to donate their time and effort to make no money. But conversely, since the aircraft (and associated missions) are owned and funded by CAP, their pilots, while not being paid per se, are effectively flying for free. There are, of course, rules associated with the program. CAP will not train pilots, so you need to have a private pilot license and be current in order to apply for the position. Upon accepting a candidate pilot, the unit will conduct a ground and air checkout. Once those are passed, a CAP pilot may fly the aircraft for which they have been approved. There is much more than can reasonably be listed here in the CAP program for pilots, so please follow the link in the references to learn more. [7]

There are a few other non-profit organizations out there that lend themselves to pilots looking for an avenue to fly. These are often geared towards youth initiatives but they are dependent upon adult participation in order to provide the services and mentorship to participating youth. Air Explorers is an excellent organization which has been around for decades. Explorers was originally a coed offshoot of Boy Scouts with posts involved in all sorts of avenues including firefighting, law enforcement, nursing, and of

---

[7] www.gocivilairpatrol.com

course, aviation. Several of these posts own and operate their own aircraft with an internal staff of instructors who are basically volunteers. But the posts also need adult volunteers who are not flight instructors to help out with leadership and administrative functions. It is very useful for these adult volunteers to be private pilots so that they may conduct orientation flights for the organization. This is a great deal for two reasons: first, you get to share your passion with those coming up behind you, and second, you will get comped for flight hours.

There are a lot of options on the table out there to break into flying. First and foremost, you have to sit down with a pen and paper and figure out just exactly what you want to get out of flying. If you want to fly for a career, then perhaps you should look at the Part 141 schools, or you may consider the military. In all honesty, this path is without any doubt the best way into an airline. There is just no other way to get paid from day 1 as a zero-time pilot and acquire the hours that airlines require. The added bonus is that all of your time, every bit of it, will be in a turbine aircraft, and if you get assigned to a medium or heavy aircraft, it will most certainly be multi-engine as well. The facts are just the facts.

If you are certain you want to fly but you are not necessarily sure of whether you want to take the plunge and do it for a living, then maybe one of the other options makes the most sense. For instance, go to a Part 61 flight school, earn a private pilot certificate, and then see about either renting, joining a flying club, or even going the CAP route. Build some hours and see how you feel about it. In my humble opinion, the CAP is a really good barometer of how professional piloting will be without requiring all of the ratings. The CAP is highly structured, having been modeled on U.S. Air Force operating procedures and doctrine. Guess who else models their flying operations similarly to military operations? The airlines! That is because a lot of their pilots are prior military aviators, so it just makes sense. The CAP will expect you to follow strict and rigid parameters for flying, and you may just decide that flying out for that infamous $100 hamburger is what you really want to get out of it. You will have a whole lot less skin in the game going this route then to go all the way through a rigorous Part 141 program just to determine that you hate flying for a living. Whatever you decide, every minute you spend researching available options is going to translate into savings down the road.

Chapter 3:
<u>Road to Wings</u>

We are now at a very critical juncture in your quest of earning wings. You have decided for any number of different reasons and factors on a mode of learning and process of earning a pilot license. No matter how far you decide to go in aviation, whether pleasure or business, it all starts with the private pilot certificate; however your training pans out and the pilot that you ultimately become all builds upon the foundation which is set right here. Every airline pilot, fighter pilot, and astronaut started somewhere. As such, it is very important to be paired with the right instructor.

This does warrant a secondary discussion about instructor selection. This may only be an option if you pursue the Part 61 route; remember, Part 141 schools are educational institutions with very specific parameters and timeframes. Also, these schools universally employ recent graduates (and current students) to conduct the flight instruction. With this in mind, the prospective candidate may end up having very little choice in the matter. This is doubly true if a candidate goes the route of the military. You have no choice in the matter, and you will suffer silently. So if you choose either of these avenues, know what to expect.

Assuming that you choose a Part 61 school, always keep in mind that you are paying the bill, the instructor works for you, and you can always take your money elsewhere. Part 61 schools are kind of a-dime-a-dozen operation and you do not need to look far to find another suiter, so plan accordingly. And always remember that everything they are teaching you is readily available and free of charge to access. Everything they are teaching you should jive with information in the Aeronautical Information Manual[8], or can be easily crosschecked with the electronic Code of Federal Regulation (eCFR)[9]. Items which are airplane specific, such as performance characteristics, can easily be crosschecked against the airplane manual. In other words, every part of the instruction process can easily be checked to ensure you are receiving quality instruction that is congruent with established rules and practices. You are paying a lot of money to learn this skillset, make sure you are getting the right service for your money.

The internet has given tremendous advantages for pilots, things that did not exist even a decade ago. For instance, when you are looking into a flight school, open up your smart phone or tablet and open up Yelp™, or any crowd-sourced review apps or websites and simply check the reviews on the flight schools that are interesting to you. This will absolutely give you the best idea of who and where offers quality services. Remember, this is a customer oriented industry and they should act accordingly. This is a changing era that we live in now, and flight schools should never see themselves as the exception.

There are a lot of things that you should look for in an instructor, but perhaps nothing more than whether or not you can get along with them. Sound over simplified? It probably does sound too easy, but seriously, this one is really important. If you don't like

---

[8]
http://www.faa.gov/air_traffic/publications/media/AIM_Basic_4-03-14.pdf
[9] http://www.ecfr.gov/cgi-bin/text-idx?tpl=/ecfrbrowse/Title14/14tab_02.tpl

you instructor, you are destined to a miserable time in the cockpit. Let me make something very clear: airplane cockpits are very small, and you will spend at least thirty hours in the cockpit with an instructor. A close friend of mine almost quit just a few hours into his license because he and the instructor really despised each other. Fortunately, he was able to work with another instructor whom he already liked on a personal level and ended up doing very well in getting his private certificate. It does sound petty, I will admit, but liking your instructor is very, very important (although it could be a very good incentive to finish your license in minimum time). If you cannot stand your instructor, it just is not very likely that you are going to get anything out of the process other than a bad taste in your mouth. Again, this goes back to seeing flight schools for what they are: a customer oriented service. When I have bad service for a $50 bill at a restaurant, they do not get my business again. Why should this same line of thinking hold true for a service that costs one hundred times as much? Why should you accept sub-par service for something with a tab of thousands of dollars? You shouldn't. Get an instructor that you like and shop around for a school with good reviews. You will be forever grateful that you did.

As with almost any vocation, the real work starts in the classroom, not the cockpit. Is it any coincidence that U.S. Air Force Undergraduate Pilot Training (UPT) begins with several weeks of classroom instruction detailing the finest minutia of aircraft specifications, operations, and emergency procedures before students ever get in the cockpit? Of course not. What you learn in the classroom can truly make or break you as a pilot. A pilot must learn to channel their naturally inquisitive nature towards things that are generally uninteresting in nature, like reading and understanding federal code.

Remember, aviation is completely ruled by bureaucracy; every little bit of aviation is governed in one way or another. This is not part of aviation (including internationally) that is not in some way spelled out and limited by federal regulation. This stuff is boring, dry, and almost universally hard to navigate. The only way to understand it is to dive into it and get to know it. If there is one thing that I would consider as a failure from my flight training experience, it would have to be how little emphasis my instructor put on studying the books. That entails everything from the aircraft operating manual to the ubiquitous FAR/AIM (Federal Aviation Regulations / Aeronautical Information Manual) that was handed us on the first day of ground school. Instead, much more emphasis was placed on studying the curriculum to pass the written test. But that is putting the cart slightly before the horse. Understanding test questions is undoubtedly important since a student pilot cannot proceed with their check ride without a passing score on the written portion. But the knowledge behind the material on the test is what is really important, and a student pilot cannot understand the weight of the question without understanding the regulatory facts driving those questions.

Ground school is exactly what the name implies: classroom study on the ground, rather than instruction in the air. There are two fairly standard ways of conducting ground school, and neither one is any more right or wrong than the other. The approach I learned from was to go through an entire year of ground school and pass the written test prior to starting the flying portion of flight training. Now the reason for this was simply because my training was conducted through a non-profit organization and the leaders of the organization wanted to ensure that the student pilots were sufficiently vested in the organization and training program before starting flight training. This was a pretty good idea given the organizational goals of teaching teenagers how to fly (which I was at the time). Given the notoriously short attention span of most teenagers, the organization did not want to flush away valuable flying hours on the trainer aircraft on student pilots who did not have the dedication to pan out. As previously mentioned, it was a non-profit organization and as such the prices were kept very low for student pilot by a lot of "sweat equity" of donations, fund raisers, and members being willing to do odd jobs and labor to make a buck. But the more student pilots there are, the more often an airplane needs downtime for maintenance (recall the 100-hour inspections required for aircraft used for instruction). I can assume that other non-profit organizations would have similar expectations.

Ground school at a Part 61 school usually is accomplished simultaneously with flight training. The theory surrounding this is that a student will spend around an hour in the classroom before taking off and then has the opportunity to practice what they learned on the ground. This idea seems to work well since thousands of people have earned their license this way. A big part of the reasoning in this also has to do with timing. Most working adults who decide to earn their license would balk at the notion of a year of classroom instruction prior to ever touching an airplane, and rightfully so. Time is money, people!

Ground school is going to be the intellectual lifeline of your flying career. All of the key knowledge that you need begins here. When you sit down to study the text, take it to heart because it will come into play in the air. Taking the time and mental energy to understand the nuances of different airspace, or approach lighting arrays, or meteorological terminology will not help you stick that perfect landing right on the numbers. It just won't. It will not help you feel more comfortable during power-on stalls and slow flight. In all reality, the mechanics of flying are simple and the basics take very little time to learn. Many student pilots conduct their first solo flight in well under ten flight hours. Think about that: a student can go from no experience to taking off and landing in an airplane by themselves in just a few hours. Obviously it is not the tactile part of flight that drives hour minimums (190 or 250 hours for commercial, etc.). It is honing those skills. It is ensuring that a pilot has the necessary understanding and experience in dealing with complex matters such as airspace, air traffic control, and emergency situations.

Ground school is the portion of flight training that does prepare you to pass the written test. So what is the written test? Technically it is the Private Pilot Knowledge test, and as the name suggests, it is just a computerized exam that tests the knowledge level of a student pilot. The body of knowledge being tested is directly out of the eCFR, §61.105 Aeronautical knowledge. As previously stated, digging into the FAR will be of great value when it comes test-time because the FAR encapsulates Title 14 of the eCFR, which is all-things regulatory relating to aviation. Areas of the exam include weight and balance, aircraft performance, navigation, weather, flight physiology, airport operations, and aircraft systems to name a few. Your ground school curriculum will cover all of the applicable areas that will be tested. When you are picking an instructor and flight school, ensure that they use a curriculum that is well-known and reputable such as Gleim®, or King Schools, Inc. There are free study guides floating around the internet and they may have some value as far as reference materials, but these reputable and established companies will provide course material that is not only proven, but also kept up to date. Federal regulation changes constantly, particularly as more technology is entered into the mix. Think about Unmanned Aircraft Systems (UAS). Following the ruling regarding these has been almost impossible since the goal posts are always moving. Put your hard earned money into a program that is professionally maintained and kept up to date.

If there is one think in your entire flying gig-bag that is going to be worth its weight in gold, it is the log book. Yes, these things are cheap, but they represent every single thing you have done as a pilot. This is unbelievably important if you intend to fly commercially, as obtaining your ratings has a lot to do with total accumulated hours, types of endorsements obtain, etc. Trust me on this one, buy a log book and treat it like gold.

In this digital age, there are a number of electronic log book options out there. Should you choose to go this route, be rather discerning in which one you decide to use especially if this is going to be your primary or sole source of logging time. Go to a reputable source like Sporty's® and pay the money for a good app like ForeFlight. Do not cheap out here, because the cost of ForeFlight and its associated subscription pales in comparison to losing out on hundreds of hours of recorded flight time.

This next section almost warrants its own chapter, but you will have plenty of time in ground school honing your skills. The topic of discussion is aeronautical charts and flight publications, or "FLIP" being the standard vernacular. This represents some of the most important components of flight planning and is absolutely one of the hardest areas of the entire ground school regimen, yet it seems to get only enough coverage to pass the portion of the test. This is just wrong. Give FLIP and charts the respect they deserve, because they can absolutely save your bacon. Knowing your navigation charts front and back may be the one thing that keeps you from having to sheepishly call a flight service station or ATC and ask them for directions because you are lost. Yes, it happens. And you will have to broadcast for the rest of the world that you cannot figure out where you are.

There are a few core flight publications that you really must become completely familiar with immediately. By immediately, this really is meant to mean immediately, because if you can decipher their cryptic meaning at your first lesson, it will do two things:

1. You will already know more about the airport you are operating from (your "home" airport) than any of the other students,

2. Impress your flight instructor to no ends.

The first little book is called the Airport/Facility Directory, and as the name suggests it contains relevant information on all public-use airports, seaplane bases and heliports, military facilities, and selected private-use facilities, military facilities, and selected private-use facilities, military facilities, and selected private-use facilities. It is published every eight weeks and is going to be the definitive guide to everything you need to know about your airport, as well as airports you will be traveling to. This does not just mean on designated cross-countries, either. There are airports all over, so unless you live in a very remote area there is probably another airport within ten to fifteen minutes which will be a nice change of pace to practice pattern work.

The A/FD should be mandatory reading for all student pilots. This is to build in them the understanding that it should be referenced every flight, and this really could not be any easier. Thanks to the wonderful folks at www.skyvector.com, a pilot can jump on the web and pull the A/FD sheet for any airport in America in .pdf format, and it is always the current edition. But why check it if you are familiar with your home airport? As previously stated, the A/FD is updated every eight weeks. The information that goes into the A/FD are items that are permanent in nature, so they will not be issued as a Notice to Airmen (NOTAM). For instance, if the Automated Weather Observation System (AWOS) frequency changes permanently, it will be updated in the A/FD and likely will not be broadcast as a NOTAM. This is important information that pilots need to know, and it is always the responsibility of the pilot-in-command to check all sources to assure safety of flight. Bear that in mind for down the road: you, as the pilot, always are the final authority on whether to go or not to go. The buck stops at you.

We need to take a look at the book now to see just what exactly it is, because words will fall short in providing an accurate depiction of what it is and does.

You will go in full-detail with this in ground school, but this is an opportunity to get a leg up beforehand. We will just focus on the basic parts of this, as a lot of the information may not be applicable to VFR pilots. I am not going to go over the entire legend, but here are the basics. The A/FD will tell you the airport designator, runway directions, length, and structural capacity, communication frequencies, weather information, runway lighting, and a remarks section which will use plain language to explain anything that the airport operator deems significant.

The first charts that student pilots are introduced to are the VFR sectional chart. It is basically a road atlas for pilots, showing different topographic variations, airspace boundaries, Special Use Airspace and restricted airspace. It also shows urban boundaries, major roads, railroad tracks, etc. These should be on your aircraft at all time given the importance of them.

Let's get out of the classroom now, and into the cockpit. The pre-planning/classroom work and references could fill a novella, and you will be fully inundated with all of it once you crack open the books. But lest we forget why you came here: you want to fly. And who could blame you? Flying is one of the great sensations in this life. There is no other feeling that can quite replicate that first time an airplane leaves the ground and you are the only person in it; it is truly unrivaled. Now that you have selected a service provider to purchase lessons from (never forget, this is still a business transaction) just what exactly is in store for you?

Your first lessons are all about the basics. Just like how you will not take a leap from elementary math to trigonometry, no one gets into an Airbus or Boeing without a few bad landings in a trainer. These first few hours of lessons are all about the basics. It starts on the ground with a thorough walk-around inspection of the airplane. Remember, you are trusting it with your life. This also establishes a pattern or behavior. If you make a habit from the very beginning of good pre-flight procedures (check the weather, NOTAMs, confirming the primary runway included) then you are that much more likely to do them every time. A huge stumbling block that is all too familiar with new pilots is radio procedures. I have never met a novice pilot who did not struggle to some extent with being comfortable on the radio, at least in the beginning. Practice is the only solution to this woe.

Once the airplane is up and running, there is a part of the process that is going to feel strange and awkward to you. This is going to be taxiing the airplane. Most trainers used are tricycle-gear configured, which is exactly as it sounds. The landing gear is a tricycle, so it feels strange at first. Also, you should get used to steering the airplane with your feet. That is not a misprint. The steering linkage is connected to the rudder pedals on the floor, so you must get used to coordinating turns using your feet. It is not very complicated, but it is nothing like driving a car. Furthermore, the brakes on most airplanes are not coordinated. This means simply that you may apply then independent of one another, and these are also usually located on the rudder pedals. You must teach your feet how to multitask, because they will be doing a bunch of different tasks from the very beginning.

Takeoffs are, quite frankly, a simple phase of flight. But this is not to say that they are not a *critical* phase of flight, because they are. Check out the NTSB accident reports; there are lots of accidents that occurred during takeoffs. There is not quite the same feeling of accomplishment on a good takeoff as there is to sticking a good landing, but in my opinion there is a little more skin in the game during takeoff. Think about it: when you land, the airplane is working with gravity. The variables involved are simply glideslope (the angle in which you are approaching the landing surface), airspeed, altitude, relative wind, and landing on the centerline. It does sound like a lot, but these all become second nature in just a few hours. Takeoffs are operating in defiance of the laws of gravity, and leaves you in a precarious situation. Your airspeed is low, the airplanes weight is high (relatively speaking; it burns fuel and loses weight from the second it is started), and your options for emergency landing are often limited. Keep your head on a swivel during takeoffs, they are very important.

The typical regimen of student pilots has very little variance from one instructor to the next. There are only a few key items that the student must be proficient in prior to soloing, so those are hit on immediately. Your very first lesson, and most of those in the first dozen hours or so, will practice the following rudimentary procedures:

- Takeoffs, landings, and traffic pattern work. To ensure that all pilots *and* air traffic controllers are on the same page, a standard traffic pattern exists which applies to every airport in the world. If you look at the airport as a road, the traffic pattern is a rectangle with rounded edges, and is comprised of four "legs". The purpose is to establish a standard procedure so that everyone in the area knows exactly where the other is in relation to the airport. The traffic pattern also has established altitudes for the same purpose.

- Ground reference maneuvers. These are Rectangular Course, S-Turns, and Turns Around a Point. These are all relatively simple maneuvers, but they take work to perfect. The idea around these is to learn how to keep a fixed distance from points on the ground as the direction of the relative wind changes as your airplane changes direction.

The Rectangular Course replicates the traffic pattern, so the point is to learn how to keep equidistance from the parameters of your rectangle. Usually, you will find a rectangular parcel of land or field, or a series of roads.

- Slow flight and stalls. This area of training teaches the low end of the performance envelope to the student, showing that an airplane will operate indefinitely at that edge of the envelope, provided the pilot does his part (maintain power, trim appropriately, etc.). Stalls simply exhibit what happens aerodynamically when the airplane drops out of the bottom of the envelope. This is a completely normal condition of every airplane, and are very important. Stalls have killed scores of pilots when they occurred during critical phases of flight (takeoff and landing), and it is important to recognize the telltale signs. Airplanes designed as trainers are engineered to be benign in all phases of flight, so slow flight and stalls are a non-event. This is not the case in high-performance airplanes; they are not meant to operate comfortably in slow flight and their slow flight and stalls can be downright unpleasant.

You will do these maneuvers over and over to prepare for solo flight; you are not expected to be a master of anything when you solo, but you must be proficient in the basics. These are the basics.

Soloing truly is a momentous occasion. While you are only considered a student pilot, a pilot who has soloed is most definitely a pilot in every sense of the word. Each instructor does preparation different for their students, and hopefully they tailor their methodology for every student. No two people react and learn in the same way. I was very blessed to have an extremely experienced instructor who also had a keen sense of people. He expressed his disdain for instructors who would just spring a solo on their students unexpectedly. As a rule of thumb, most people do not react well to this sort of thing. The exception to this rule would be the student who is very unsure of themselves and has, for instance, twenty or more hours of flying and just does not have the confidence to solo. These folks probably need that nudge, with the instructor asking to pull off the taxiway to "check something", and then stepping out of the airplane. My instructor, and all the good ones I know, methodically laid out in the lessons leading up to soloing exactly what to expect. In my experience, my CFI eased away from ground reference maneuvers and slow flight and stalls in the two or three hours leading up to my solo, and we focused strictly on pattern work[10]. The day of my solo, my CFI told me he planned to have me solo, what he planned to do (i.e., pull off the runway and taxi to the hangar to drop him off), and then we took off together and flew in the pattern for about thirty minutes together. He instructed me to conduct three circuits in the pattern, two being touch-and-goes and the third to a full stop. Since he went over the whole process meticulously beforehand, my nerves were not on edge and my solo was textbook. This goes back to selecting

---

[10] In this sense, "pattern work" refers to the cycle of takeoff, flying the traffic pattern completely, and landing. Generally, pattern work means the pilot intends to do numerous circuits in the pattern. Each landing may either be a full-stop landing, or the touch-and-go, in which they touch down, rollout a short distance, and advance the throttle to takeoff back into the pattern again.

your instructor in chapter 2; make sure that you hire someone that you get along with and trust.

Soloing is unbelievably rewarding, and you are now going to be in a very small and exclusive group of people. Pilots make up the vast minority of the population, so you will become part of a very close-knit group. Pilots love being pilots, and would usually rather talk about flying than just about anything else.

Once you solo, this type of flying will become a big part of the total time towards your private pilot certificate, with a 10-hour minimum requirement flying solo, five of that being cross-country. Perhaps the greatest thrill at this point in your training (besides soloing) is going to be flying at night. Night flying is absolutely wonderful, particularly with a large moon. When it is all boiled down, flying is all about taking in our surroundings to the greatest extent. Sure, we have turned it into a thriving global market, as well as a critical component of national defense, but that was not what fueled Man's desire to fly for unknown generations.

There is not much left with the license after cross-country work, because that takes up most of the flight hours after you solo. The rest is comprised of a few hours "under the hood", which is flying on instruments, and then prep work for the check ride. Probably the most important piece of advice that can be offered is to do this process of earning your certificate in the fastest way possible. You will not retain much of the motor skills used in flight if they are not routinely practiced, which will lead to more flight hours having to be devoted to basic maneuvers. There is nothing wrong with getting back to the basics; all pilots should just go practice the simple stuff occasionally. But the purpose of flying lessons is to obtain a license, not practice simple maneuvers endlessly. Believe it or not, pilots are more than welcome to go out and brush up on simple maneuvers *after* being awarded their license, so moving towards the goal of getting the license would be the high priority.

Chapter 4:
<u>After your check ride</u>

The best piece of advice that I ever received in flying was also the most simple: strive to learn something new every time you fly. You will have mastered the most difficult aspect of the learning curve if you commit yourself to that one idea, and that is beating out complacency. Even just a few short flight hours after soloing, basic pattern work feels mundane, even though student pilots have far from mastered even basic maneuvers. So the first thing a freshly minted private pilot should do (after the requisite flights with family and friends) is...practice some more.

The private pilot license is probably one of two things: a license to learn, or a means-to-and-end. However, if it is the end-result of your flying ambition, i.e., you desire to go no further, than it should still be a license to learn every time you get in the cockpit. Or open up your favorite flying website. Or check the Meteorological Terminal Aviation Routine Weather Report (METAR) and Terminal Aerodrome Forecast (TAF) just because you can, not because you plan to fly that day. Get the gist of where this is going? Learning something every day about flying does not mean that learning only comes to you in the cockpit or in the briefing rooms. This is especially true with the plethora of aviation-specific websites and mobile apps out there. It is so easy to just open one of these for a few minutes and learn something. For instance, open up the airport diagram of your home station and study it for 10 minutes. Make mental notes of all the taxiways, where they cross runways, and what the dominant routes are to the primary runway from where you generally taxi from. The next time you fly, a new found confidence will emerge because you will spend less time second-guess where that taxiway crosses the runway that you always forget about since the markings and signs are faded and dingy. Check out on the same diagram if there are any Hot Spots on your airport, and read why they are designated as such. Use a search engine and find a METAR/TAF decoder and study it, so the next time you actually need to check the weather to fly, you will not need to pull of the decoder to figure out what the weather says. Pull out your E6B and search for some practice problems online. Practice determining weight and balance based on the airplane you are checked out in. Go to SkyVector or DUATS, create a flight plan, and then cross-check it against physical charts. This stuff is so accessible, and anything you have questions on are on the web. Most schools with aviation programs have dedicated YouTube channels with dozens of free videos on these sorts of things, and if it a professional channel (Embry-Riddle, AOPA, FAA, EAA, etc.) you can bet the information is legitimate and accurate.

Beyond this point, the choice is really up to you. There are a bunch of different ways you can go with this, but the most important point is to go out and have fun with it. Flying should never just be another day at the office. It is something so much bigger than that. I have never regretted the decision to forgo the Professional Pilot program at a prominent aviation program that was offered to me almost one decade ago. All of the graduates of that program that I know (and that amounts to a couple of dozen, at least) have regretted it because of the enormous cost coming out of it, and the very low pay to be expected upon first hire. The caveat to this were the graduates of the program that were accepted as military pilots; they all started out making very good pay comparatively in the uniform.

But that lifestyle is not for everybody, and the vetting process is extremely rigorous. Besides, the military routinely accepts applicants for flight training that have no flying experience at all, so the question there begs why do the flying program if it really does not make a difference? But I digress. If you love it enough and want to do it for a career, then you will find a way to make it work. There is no iron-clad roadmap to success in flying; it is up to you to determine what success means to you. If proving to yourself that you can face your fears, follow your dream, and earn a private pilot license is the epitome of success and you achieve that, then you have succeeded. If being a Captain of a Boeing 777 on intercontinental routes is your dream, you can achieve that, too, but it will take a long time to get there and a lot of grit. But you can do it. The only one who can hold you back from it is you.

A theme that emerged earlier in this book is the flying community. If it is nothing else, it is absolutely a close-knit community. For you to get the most out of your time in the air, you really need to figure out where you fit in the community. If there is one thing that I know about this thing called flying, it is that networking is king. That is not just directed toward the prospective careerist; every pilot needs to determine their place in the order. There is no better way to do this than just jumping right in. Every FBO that I have been too has a stack of flying magazines and newsletters, most of which have upcoming events, aka, fly-ins. Look at the list, find one (or more), rent an airplane and go there. Do you have an interest in building and flying one of the Vans RV-series kit planes? Those communities are very robust and have usually have a number of fly-ins. Yes, your cool-factor will be in the negative figures when you show up in that tired rental C-172, but showing the initiative to just be there, asking questions, showing interest (authors note: if you pay the money to rent an airplane to fly to a fly-in for an type of airplane that you do not own, the owners will recognize this. As long as you seem legitimate, they will likely share their community with you hardily) and asking questions, you will go a long way towards establishing your identity in the community. This is just an example of course, but a valid one.

Fly-ins are the bread-and-butter of the community. They are centered around two things all pilots agree on: flying and food. By attending these (preferably attending by flying), you will gain a great footing in the community. You will meet like-minded people who share similar interests at the very least.

Chapter 5:
So, you want to fly for money?

This topic was touched on earlier in book, but it deserves its own chapter because to be perfectly honest, how many aspiring pilots *don't* get into it with at least a passing interest in doing it as a profession? There are several basic routes that an aspiring pilot can go to fly professionally, so I will cover the most prolific of those.

Perhaps one of the most cherished positions in any branch of the military are the pilots. These guys have it all; they get great nicknames and have copious movies made just for them. What a great deal! Of course, those movies rarely depict exactly how grueling the training is, how touch the competition is to get a slot, and how much effort goes into maintaining proficiency and upgrading throughout a career. The ballpark estimate of cost to train on U.S. Air Force pilot is over $1 million. These positions are sacred for a reason, and it behooves the branches of service to scrutinize judiciously who ends up in the cockpit of their aircraft.

On the other hand, I personally have known several dozen military pilots, so of them quite close, and can assure you that there is nothing particularly special about most of them. Yes, a couple of them have highly technical degrees in astrophysics or engineering, but these have been generally the exception rather than the rule. The point is, you do not need to major in aeronautical engineering to get a look by the military. What you need is a really strong work ethic, excellent references, and a good GPA. Majoring in something that you can earn a high GPA in is actually important, perhaps more important than the actual major.

If your goal is military flying, there are a million nuances to understand in determining which direction to follow. There is really no single deciding factor in the decision making process for military flying because all of the branches of service use aviation in different ways. Even within each branch of service, there are a number of different missions.

The Air Force owns the role of air superiority, close air support, and heavy transport. The name of the game for Air Force missions is a deeply centralized mission, and their aircraft operate in large wings stationed at hub-style airfields. As a rule of thumb, Air Force assets rarely operate out of forward operating bases or austere conditions. Rather, they take large support packages with them wherever they go. This makes for rather predictable operations (for most of their missions; there are certainly exceptions).

The Air Force also offers several options in becoming a pilot in the form of three distinctly different components of the branch. Before you discount this as minutia, it is very important if you are considering the Air Force route. This route is appealing because, as the name suggests, they have the Lion's share of flying positions in the military. The Air Force is broken down into three distinct components:

1. Active Duty. This is the bulk of the Air Force asset base.

2. Reserves. Traditionally a "part-time' component, but falls under the command of the active duty.

3. Air National Guard. The second reserve component of the Air Force, much larger that the Air Force Reserve. The primary difference between the two is that the Air National Guard

does not fall under the command of the active duty Air Force.

Each of the three components of the Air Force have pilot billets, and there are annual quotas that must be met for sustainment sake. The age cutoff is the candidate must start pilot training before their 30th birthday, and this is rather hard to get waived. So what exactly are the benefits of each one? It depends on what you are looking for. If you want to leave the selection of which airframe you will fly to the discretion of the Air Force, and you want the security of a full-time job from the get-go, then the active duty is probably the way that you will want to go. Of course, this leaves you open to some of the less desirable locations such as Minot, North Dakota, or Clovis, New Mexico. But there certainly is something to be said for job security, I suppose.

While the Air Force Reserve has a small smattering of stand-alone units, or Wings, the bulk of their flying missions are actually attached to active duty wings. The reserve supplies aircrew and maintainers, utilizing active duty jets. In this way, they really are under the thumb of the active duty leadership. But if you primary interest is flying, and no the politics that come with the organizations, then this should be of little consequence. Unlike the active duty, one key advantage of the reserve components is that the prospective pilot applies for a specific position in a particular unit, so there is no surprise where you will be assigned, or what airframe you will be flying.

The Air National Guard is perhaps the most flexible of the three. The Guard is structured completely differently than the Reserve. Every state has its own guard contingents, generally comprised of at least one flying wing, with larger states often having several stand-alone wings. In this sense, you have the greatest advantage of finding a mission and location that fits your desires and needs. Here is a little insider trading information: Alaska has several Guard flying missions, and they have a notoriously difficult time filling their pilot billets. They recruit out-of-state aggressively, often offering incentives that other states cannot or will not offer to prospective pilot candidates. This is not to say that you will be a shoe in, but if you know the ins and outs, and possess a willingness to move to the work, then your odds may be greatly improved. The primary detractor in this scenario is that Guard units cannot guarantee full-time employment, so the units in Fairbanks in particular really struggle to pull in candidates because most people are not willing to move up to the edge of the wilderness with very few prospects for work to be a part-time pilot. It all comes down to how much risk you are willing to take if this is something you really want to do. Air Force wings of silver are exactly the same whether your contract says active duty, reserve, or guard.

The U.S. Army possesses what I consider to be the most sensible solution in creating pilots: the bulk of their pilot candidates are Warrant Officers, a rank structure strictly dedicated to the craft of flying without the burden of command responsibility that comes with a commission. The candidates are farmed out of the enlisted corps of troops, so the potential picks have a familiarity with the order and discipline of military life already. This makes the vetting process much more secure, in my opinion, as there are people inside the organization already who may either vouch for their character, or provide cautionary advice against them. Also, the Army method tends to shy away the issue of overgrown egotism which has plagued its sister-service of Air Force for generations. But being prior-enlisted is not the only option with the Warrant Officer program; you may apply directly for the program as young as 18 years of age with no previous military experience, or a college degree (four-year degrees are only mandatory for commissioned officers; the Warrant Officer program has no collegiate obligation). This, perhaps, reflects the utilitarian view that the Army holds on its Aviation Branch. From my own personal experience, aviators are no more significant in the Army force structure than artillery men or armor; indeed, the Army looks at aviation more as a logistics support branch. Depending on the applicant's temperament, this may work in their favor. Aviators may generally fly under the radar in the ranks of the Army, whereas their profile is much higher in the Air Force.

The only drawback (and it does not have to be a drawback) to Army aviation is the centricity around rotary aircraft. This is not to say that the Army operates no fixed-wing aircraft, in fact they have dozens. But all Army aviators start their careers in helicopters, and this may not be helpful depending upon your career aspirations down the road. If after a career in the military your wish is to fly wide-body jets transoceanic, a career of flying cargo helicopters VFR at 50'off the ground will not translate well. If you want to fly life flight helicopters, then this background is probably perfect.

The Army, like the Air Force, has three components which all offer pilot billets. The National Guard of every state has Army National Guard aviation assets, so there is potential no matter where you live should you prefer the part-time route.

The Army Reserve, unlike the Air Force Reserve, generally stands in small units nationwide. For what they do, helicopters have a much smaller logistic footprint than Air Force flying wings, so they are easy to place at municipal airports around the country, rather than as a tenant of an active duty unit.

The active duty component of the Army is not much different than the Air Force, conceptually anyway. It is certainly not a bad deal, as the pay for a military pilot is excellent from day one as compared to that of a rookie commercial pilot. But as with all things, there are tradeoffs.

For the purposes of this book, the Navy, U.S. Marine Corps, and Coast Guard will all be looked as one entity. The nuances are too subtle for those unacquainted with military culture to make a difference. It is important to remember when considering becoming a military pilot that the aviation branch of each respective branch of service exists to support whatever the core mission of that service is. For the Army, that is close-in, direct support of combat arms soldiers, which is why their fleet consists mostly of helicopters and their tactics are structured around that. For the Air Force, the mission is providing top cover for all other missions, and then the rest is purely support functions. Hate to burst your bubble flyboys, but that is the truth. The Navy's primary role is supremacy over the seas, so their aviation branch is geared to provide just that. The Navy aviation fleet is not particularly diverse, relying on just a few airframes to cover a wide array of missions. The Navy flying mission is not for the faint of heart; by design, they are expected to operate off the deck of a ship only marginally larger than a football field, in all weather conditions, and most of their work is over the unforgiving open water. Their missions are short-range in nature and are intended for two purposes:

1. Air defense of the fleet.

2. A rapid-response package giving the U.S. quick-strike capability of a moderate air package within hours, rather than weeks.

The other air missions in the Navy basically consist of short-haul cargo, mine-sweeping and anti-submarine, search-and-rescue, and airborne warning and command-and-control.

The Navy and Marines both have reserve units, but not nearly on the same scale as the Air Force and Army reserve components. If you wish to fly Navy, active duty is probably going to be the most favorable way to go for your own sake.

In a perfect world, a person who wishes to become a military pilot has nothing more to do than ask and they could have their pick of which branch of service, which mission, and which airframe they wished to choose from. That is not the real world, though. You may not be able to afford being choosy if you wish to earn military wings. It may behoove you to saturate the market, applying for every branch of service, active-duty and reserve components alike. Assuming you do have the ability to be picky, then a lot of this comes down to personal preference. There are a lot of things to consider. For the Army, aviation units are deployed to the field just like their combat arms brethren, for just as long (usually a year). The Navy and Marines are expected to go out to see for long tours (six months); it is the nature of the beast. The Air Force has the most variety in this matter, because so much depends on the airframe. For instance, if you were assigned to a fighter-bomber mission, you will deploy as part of a large package to operate from a fixed base, usually for six months. However, if you happen to be assigned to the prime movers like the C-17A or the C-5A/M, you will not deploy as a unit. Instead, you will spend most of your year gone on short trips (ten days or so). During the height of Iraqi Freedom, C-5 Galaxy aircrews were averaging over 200 days per year away from home, despite never once being officially "deployed".

Having the military pick up the tab and pay you to fly can be fantastic, but always beware that nothing is free. Each branch of service has minimum service obligations set aside just for pilots since the cost to produce a pilot is so high. I believe the going rate is a ten-year commitment, so recognize that in the event you change your mind and wish to go a different direction in life away from the military, that may be a lot easier said than done. But the flip side of the coin is that the military pilot continues to build time in the cockpit over those years that they are obligated to serve, and those hours are invaluable for the individual with aims of flying for the airlines. If you have the stomach to stay in the military and put up with it, it can be a good deal. The pay really is quite competitive up until about mid-career, which would be when a military pilot would be on par in hours with civilian pilots who are coming eligible to upgrade to captain from first officer. But for young pilots, there is absolutely no comparison in both pay and benefits, but also in quality of life and time behind the yoke.

Having extrapolated the military option, let us move on to some of the other options. The most prolific type of piloting is always going to be airline pilots, and the demand is most certainly there. Boeing estimates a demand for over 600,000 pilots worldwide through 2035[11], so there will be ample opportunity to enter this

---

[11] http://www.boeing.com/commercial/market/long-term-

trade. The problem is that the FAA is not helping matters at all in getting those seats filled; in July of 2013 they passed a mandate dramatically upping the minimum standards that first officers must have before holding that position. Previously to the mandate, a first officer could hold the position with a minimum of 250-hours and a commercial certificate. These credentials are relatively easy to obtain compared to the new, amended standards. The current minimum requirement now stands at 1,500-hours and an ATP rating. This is a huge stumbling block due to the enormous cost of accumulating that much time in the cockpit. It stands to reason that first officers accumulate time rather quickly and learn accordingly, which is why the 250-hour threshold had worked for quite a long time. This appears to have been a knee-jerk reaction by the FAA to fix a safety problem which never was. While the bureaucrats of the FAA high-fived over this powerful "safety" regulation[12], the industry heaved a collective groan. They know the cost to reach that threshold, and people just do not fly 1,500 hours in the hope of making $30,000 per year to fly the right seat. You can make that much as an Uber driver taking people to the airport.

With this restriction securely in place, there are going to be only a few options to supply the necessary pilots. North America constitutes about 17% of that pie of future pilot needs, with about 112,000 total expected. It is difficult to determine where those will all come from, but the first well to tap is usually departing military pilots. They are experienced, cool under

---

market/pilot-and-technician-outlook/
[12]

https://www.faa.gov/news/press_releases/news_story.cfm?newsId=148
38

pressure, and are very well trained. Also, military pilots generally have exclusively turbine-engine time, often with multi-engine time as well. But airlines cannot bank on this as a reliable and steady source of pilots; the military does not mint pilots for the benefit of anyone but the military. It calls the shots about how many they create and those selected to fly are beholden to their rules for a prescribed period of time.

About the only reasonable way to get the hours necessary for a jump to the "bigs" besides the military is as a Certified Flight Instructor. These jobs are usually in high demand, and for a good reason: the turnover rate is very high in them. There are basically two types of flight instructors out there: young pilots shooting for the moon, and old retired types who don't want a real job anymore. Unfortunately, the former is much more prevalent. Flight instructor is, quite frankly, not a career-oriented track. The pay is low, the job is very demanding, and the hours are awful. After all, most working-class adults taking lessons do so when *they* are off work. CFIs notoriously work evenings, weekends, and any other time that the rest of the 9-to-5 crowd are off work. But it is one of very few commercial flying gigs that is readily available to low-time pilots. The other ones are basically niche gigs that are difficult to get into for other reasons, but I will get into that later in this book. There is not much more to elaborate on with flight instructing as a vocation; it has been a long-standing understanding that if you did not go the military route, this is how you get the hours to get your foot in the door. It is my prediction that this will become ever truer in the coming years. Also, I foresee a scramble for military billets regardless of international affairs as aspiring pilots realize just how difficult a task it will be to obtain the requisite 1,500 hours.

Corporate flying is a sector of the market that is tried and true, assuming a pilot can get their foot in the door. The charter market should continue to grow on a commensurate rate as the rest of commercial air travel, so there will be jobs here. Google for pilot jobs and you will get a list of sites posting aviation jobs and pilot jobs, and there is certainly opportunity in the charter market. However, much of these require not just x-amount of hours, but also a type-rating in whichever aircraft they need pilots for. Obtaining type ratings for jets is costly, so it is not as though Joe Pilot is going to go collect type ratings for Learjet's, Citations, or Hawker jets just because. If you happen to have a type rating for a Beech King Air 90, but the jobs need some other type rating, you might just be out of luck, or have to sign a promissory contract stating you will obtain the type-rating in a certain time period.

Just looking at common job search engines like Indeed or Monster yield a bunch of hits for current openings, but be forewarned: they are not looking for junior pilots. For instance, a major retailer posted a job for a first officer for their corporate fleet and had a 3,500 hour minimum requirement, with 2,000 as pilot-in-command, and 1,500 in turbine aircraft. And this is for the co-pilot. The other charter/corporate jobs had similar requirements.

So just what exactly can you do with a commercial license and 250 hours? There are still a couple of options out there if you are not really interested in instructing. Once again, the internet saves the day. A quick search yields some interesting prospects, such as aerial surveying, ferrying, and short-haul passenger chartering (which does not fall under FAA's minimum hour mandate). However, a lot of these jobs only offer part-time pay and benefits.

The honest-to-goodness most realistically profitable form of commercial flying might come as a surprise, but it lies out in the vast heartlands of America. Agriculture pilots, or "crop dusters", are in a constant demand and always will be as long as people continue to eat food. This is not easy work, the flying is low, bumpy, and hot (you only apply to crops during the growing season, i.e., spring and summer). You will not get picked up straight out of flight school, as you have to obtain certain licenses to work with the chemicals, and you will probably start out working for an outfit as part of the ground crew cadre, fueling airplanes and loading them with their payload. This flying is not for everyone, and you will have to go where the work is. This is basically the entire longitudinal central region on the United States, stretching from the deltas of Mississippi and Louisiana, through Texas, and straight north all the way to Canada through the plains states. California is an agricultural hub, and as such has a thriving ag flying population. Also, the climate is temperate so you can fly a lot.

If this type of flying interests you, there are some addendums that must be met. First, you must be tailwheel endorsed, as all ag airplanes are tailwheel configured. Second, you must be licensed in the state(s) you will be working in to handle pesticides. If you plan to be a migratory pilot and move across the states throughout the year, you will need to obtain license in all states (unless states you wish to work in offer reciprocity with each other). There are several schools that specialize in training specifically for this industry, and offer job placement services. This will be a costly, so make sure this is something that you are really passionate about and want to do. This is still a grassroots part of the aviation industry and affords options that otherwise may not be available. According to the National Agriculture Aviation Association[13], there may still be opportunities to get onboard as part of a ground crew and become an apprentice, ultimately being groomed by the chief pilot to become a pilot. This is an old-school method of vesting candidates, which is extremely valuable to these operations. It dramatically reduces the risk of going bust on a pilot by hiring strictly off of credentials alone. There is no guarantee that ag operations will offer this, but it might certainly be worth the while to try. There are few other opportunities, if any, in flying that afford this sort of experience. It would be useful to do this anyway just to be around commercial aviation to see if it is even something that you want to devote so much in to. The odds are much better in these operations of being noticed by the flying staff than working as a ramp hand for an airline; those will just be dead-end, labor-intensive jobs with no possible avenue into the cockpit. Working on an ag team may.

The outlook for becoming a pilot is, quite honestly, not very inviting. There is a major disconnect between the growing demand for pilots and any efficient method of getting them there. To be perfectly frank, if you plan to break into commercial flying through any of the routes mentioned (besides the military), you really need to have a second job lined up. Most of them only start around $20,000-$30,000 per annum, and a lot of these jobs may only be seasonal or part-time. That being said, the cockpit is not the only career path in aviation. It has certainly the most risk, and the turnover rate is rather high for inexperienced first officers. They find that they can do a lot of other jobs outside of aviation that pay better without the backbreaking requirements that pilots must uphold. In the long run, if a pilot is able to

---

[13] http://www.agaviation.org/

stick with it and gain seniority, the job becomes very lucrative. But the road is long and winding to get there, and a lot of people drop off along the way.

Mechanics are a growing demand, and will continue to be so throughout the next two decades. Boeing predicts a market demand of 118,000 new technicians through 2035[14] for North America, and even greater demand in Europe and Asia. Becoming a technician may be a very prudent career path to follow; there is job security in it, and the training is much less costly than pilot training. FAA-approved Airframe & Powerplant (A&P) courses are offered at community colleges and vocational schools all across the country[15], so students should not have to travel very far to find one. Tuition is usually quite low at these schools so you can walk away in less than two years ready to join the workforce, for a cost that could reasonably be paid out of pocket or as-you-go. With a median income of $61,020[16], the pay is very livable. The basic caveat is that the work is where airports are; you will not find many jobs if you are dying to live in the wild country of Wyoming or Montana.

If you prefer non-technical route (or just do not care to work in the great outdoors), there are a few career paths that are in constant demand. Airport operations is a field that was once filled mostly be former pilots, but is now becoming recognized as its own unique vocation, with formal academic training being offered at some of the most prominent aviation programs in the nation. The median income is fairly

---

[14] http://www.boeing.com/commercial/market/long-term-market/pilot-and-technician-outlook/

[15] http://www.aviationschoolsonline.com/school-listings/aircraft-maintenance-schools/2.php

[16] http://www.bls.gov/oes/current/oes493011.htm

good at $52,360[17], but the shear law of averages shows that there is going to be a lot less opportunity overall doing this as opposed to becoming a technician or pilot, with just under 8,000 positions nationwide in 2015, as opposed to the approximately 124,000 maintenance technicians. Also, it has been my experience that most airport operations jobs prefer the candidate to have a commercial rating and instrument rating. Also, smaller operations at regional airports (non-hub commercial airports) generally expect the airport ops staff to have or earn basic aircraft rescue and firefighting credentials as they will be the rescue staff. These jobs usually pay significantly lower than either working for the government or at a major hub airport, but they will be your first opportunity to break into this market if you wish to pursue this route. It is really the opposite of a maintenance technician; in those you would not want to be relegated to minor airports, as there is no future at those locations. For airport operations, this is most likely the only way to break into the market.

Air Traffic Control is perhaps the most ubiquitous aviation job outside of the cockpit, and pulls into the final position in the careers portion of this book. This job has been at the center stage of controversy in the past, but relatively little is known about it as they are most certainly out of sight and out of mind. What is commonly known is that it tops the charts of most stressful vocations, and the pay is good. That pretty well sums it up in a nutshell I suppose. ATC does pay well, but you must get on board first. When the FAA opens up hiring, it is done en masse, no experience necessary. The FAA has a training academy where they internally train all new hires.

---

[17] http://www.bls.gov/oes/current/oes532022.htm

If you are interested in ATC, it is important to understand the division of labor. The FAA controls all of the Air Route Traffic Control Centers, or "centers", as well as most towered airports. However, some control towers are contractors, so there is opportunity outside of the FAA if you wish to pursue that route. However, you will need to be qualified to get a look from the contract agencies. There are numerous colleges offering ATC majors now, so you can certainly get the training from them. Personally, I would just enlist in the military guaranteed placement in ATC; all branches of service have ATC so the opportunity is there.

Appendix:
Resources for Beginners

Without being longwinded here, there are a few must-reads for all prospective pilots, and established pilots alike. The first, and it really should be read cover-to-cover, is the FAAs Aeronautical Information Manual. As previously mentioned, it is the comprehensive catalog of all things flying. This is required reading through the private pilot program, but you should get the drop on it and read it ahead of time. It is free on the FAA website as a .pdf file, so no need to wait and purchase it.

The AOPA is the definitive resource for all pilots, so just go ahead and consider a membership with them a fixed expense in your flying budget. They are the organization that carriers the most weight lobbying for pilots, and a membership with them unlocks an unbelievable amount of web content and tools on their fantastic website.

If your interests delved at all into ultralights, light sports, warbirds, or experimental aircraft, then you are going to need to join the Experimental Aircraft Association. This organization is very large and lobbies hard for these categories of aviation. How big is the EAA? Well, they put on the world-famous Oshkosh Air Venture annually, so pretty big. Even if you do not plan to operate in the aforementioned types of flying, this group is still a good one to join.

Commonly Websites:

1. http://www.faa.gov
2. http://www.icao.int
3. http://www.aopa.org
4. http://www.eaa.org
5. http://www.airnav.com
6. http://www.skyvector
7. http://www.duats.com
8. http://www.flightaware.com
9. http://www.faa.gov/air_traffic/publications/media/AIM_Basic_4-03-14.pdf
10. http://www.aviationweather.gov

Flight School Links:

1. http://www.erau.edu
2. http://polytechnic.k-state.edu/aviation/
3. https://atpflightschool.com/
4. http://www.flightsafety.com/
5. http://www.spartan.edu
6. http://aviation.und.edu/
7. http://www.ucmo.edu/aviation
8. http://ocm.auburn.edu/aviation_center/
9. http://www.flightschoollist.com
10. http://technology.asu.edu/aviation/

Professional Organizations:

1. https://www.nbaa.org/
2. http://www.naa.aero/
3. http://www.nata.aero/

Made in the USA
Monee, IL
09 January 2021